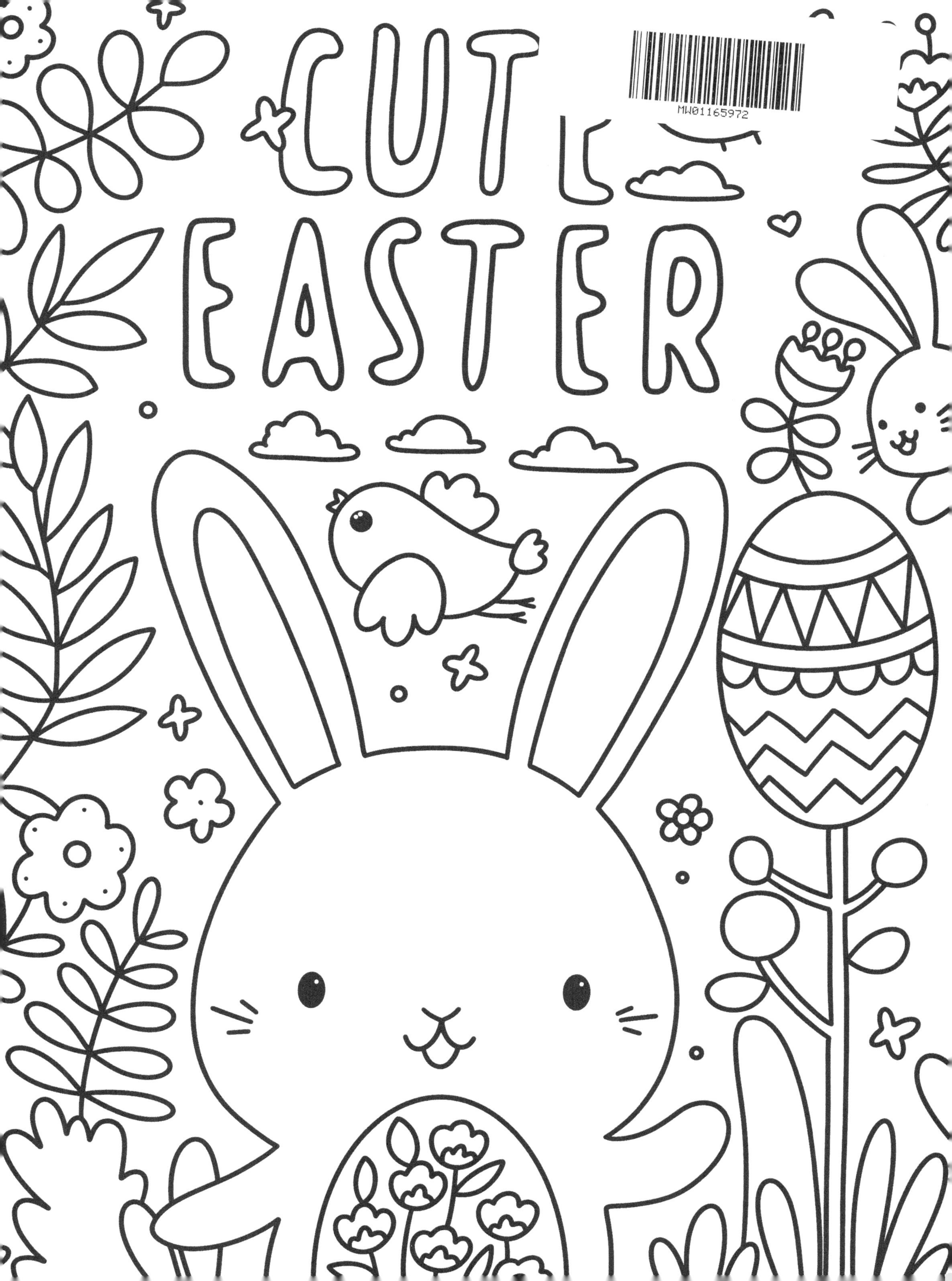
CUT
EASTER

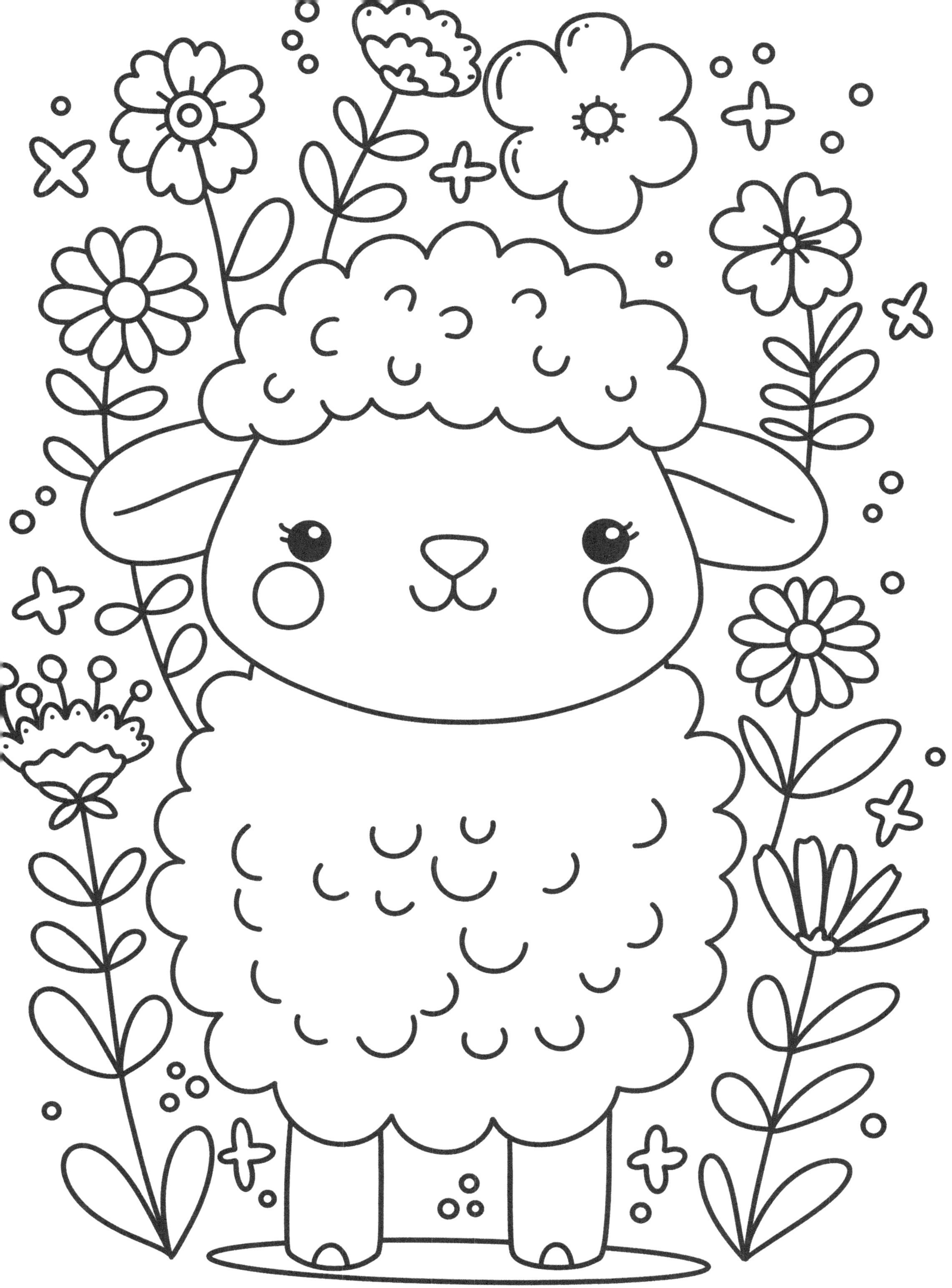

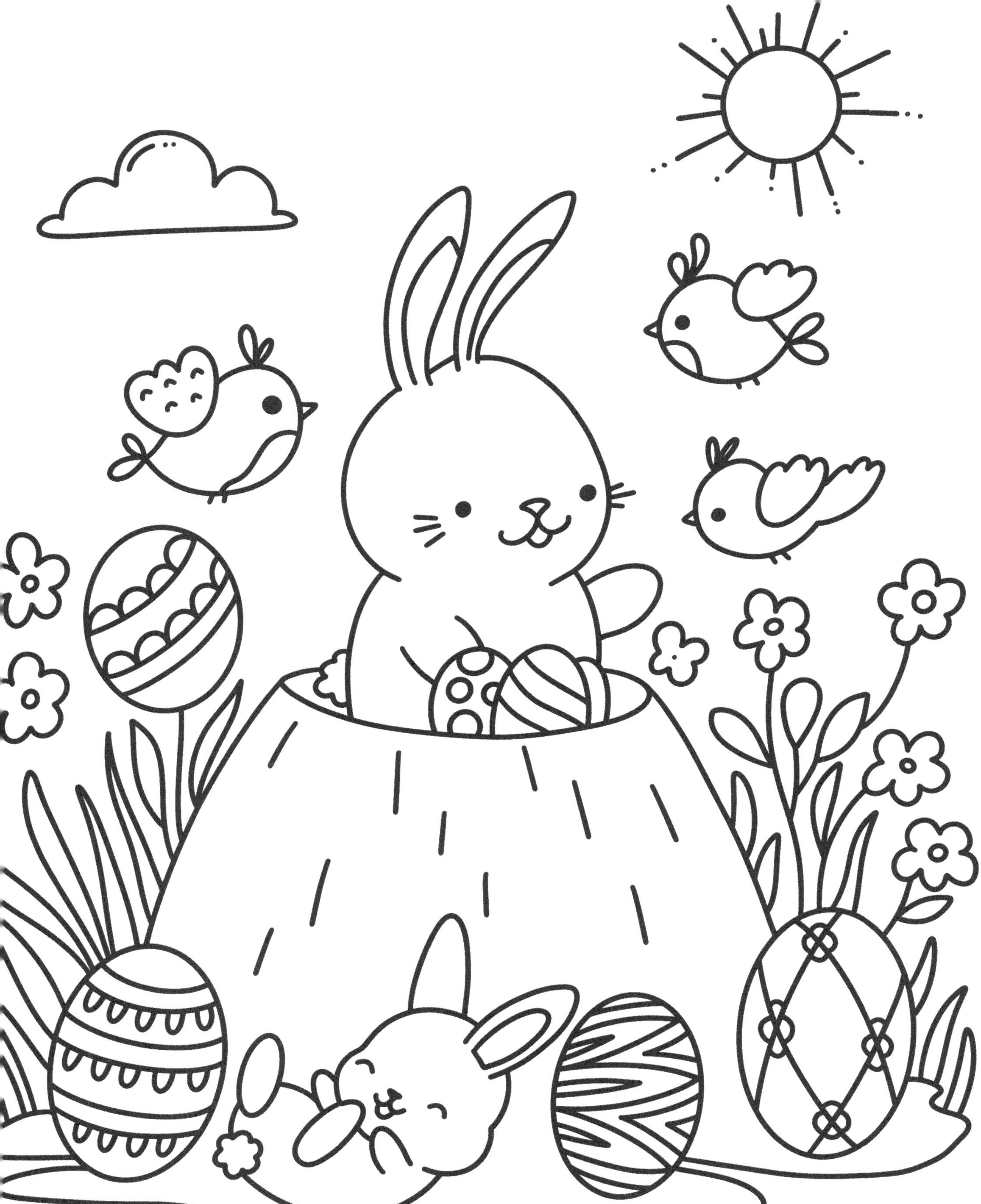

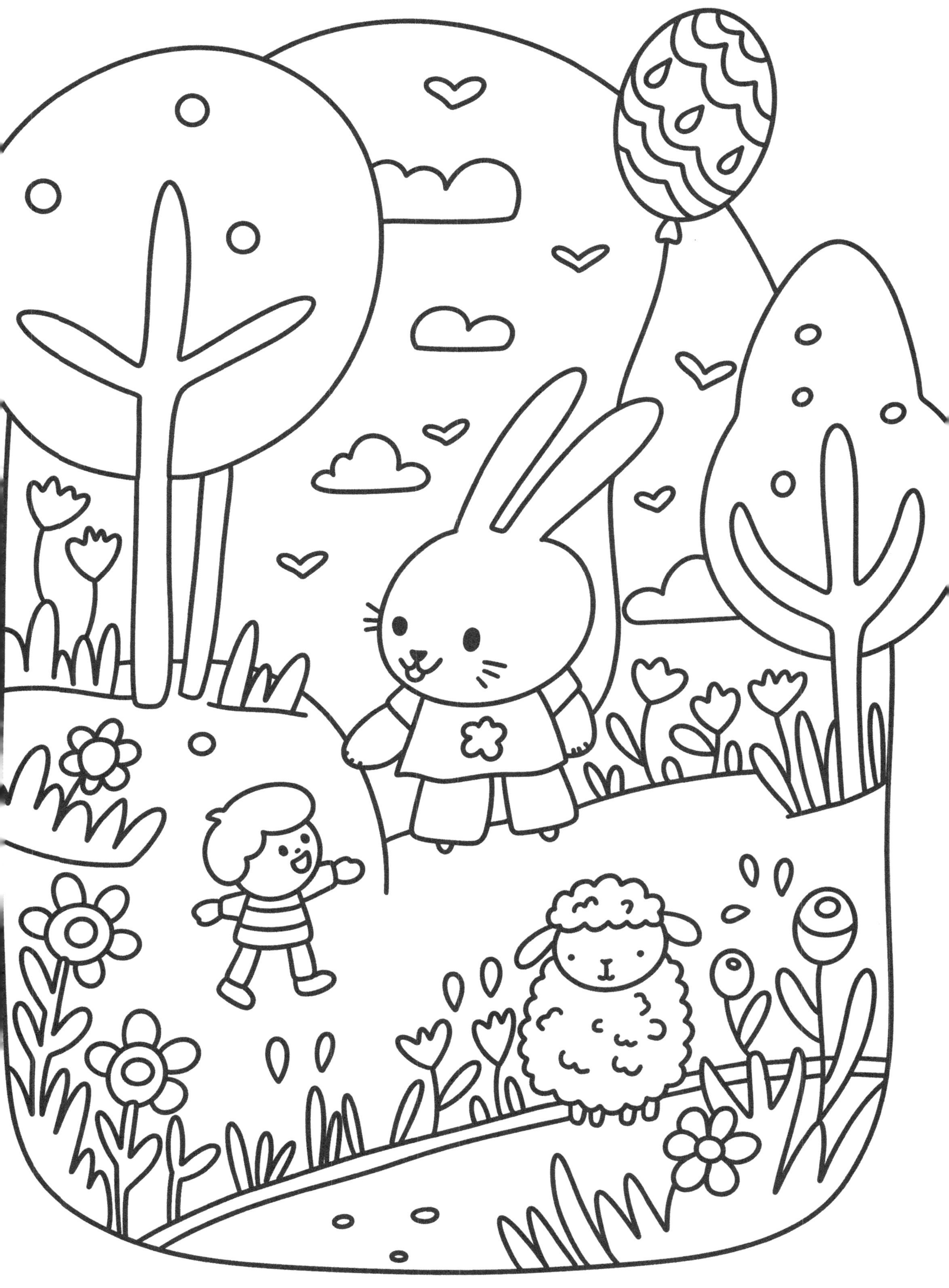

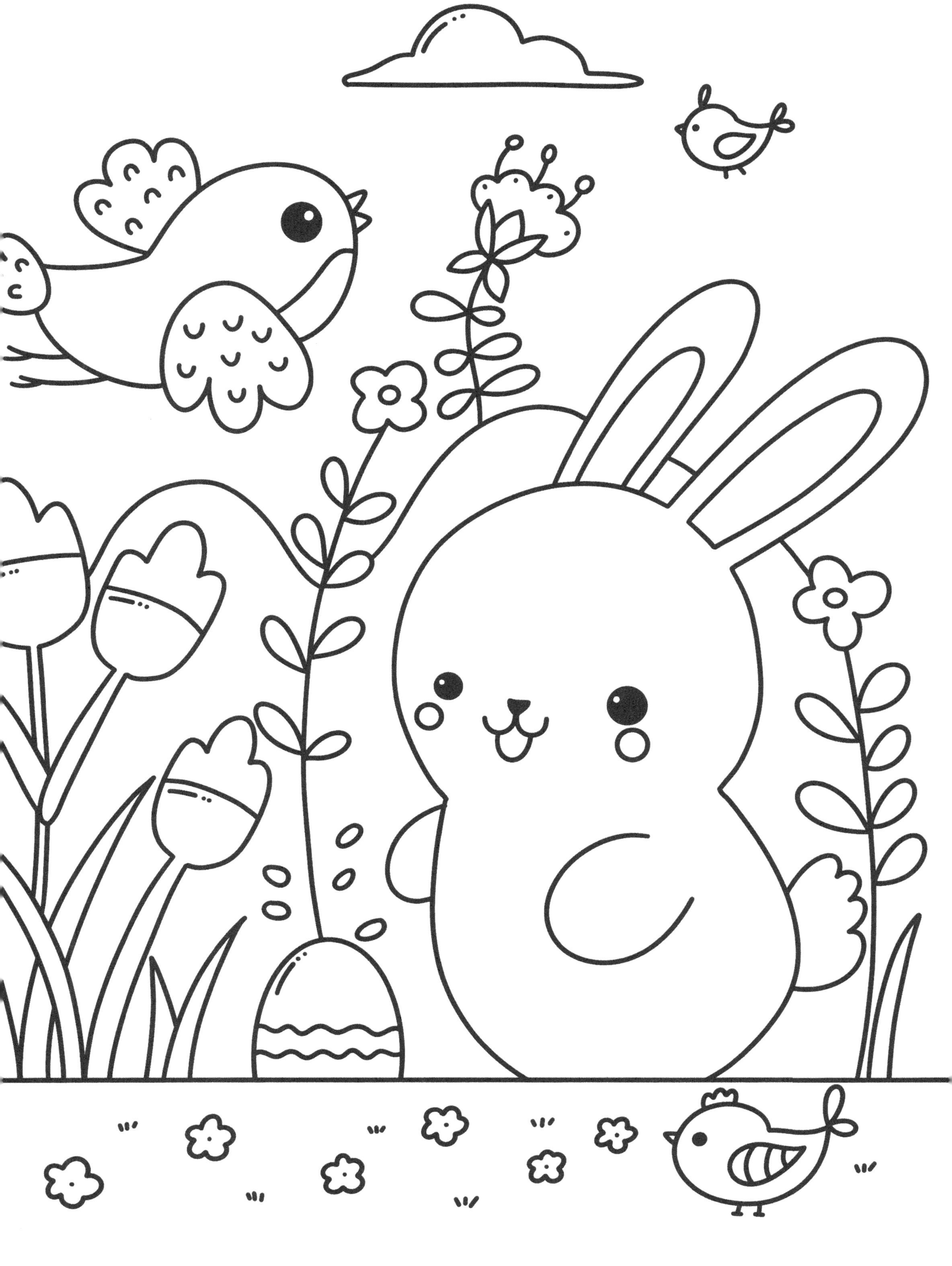

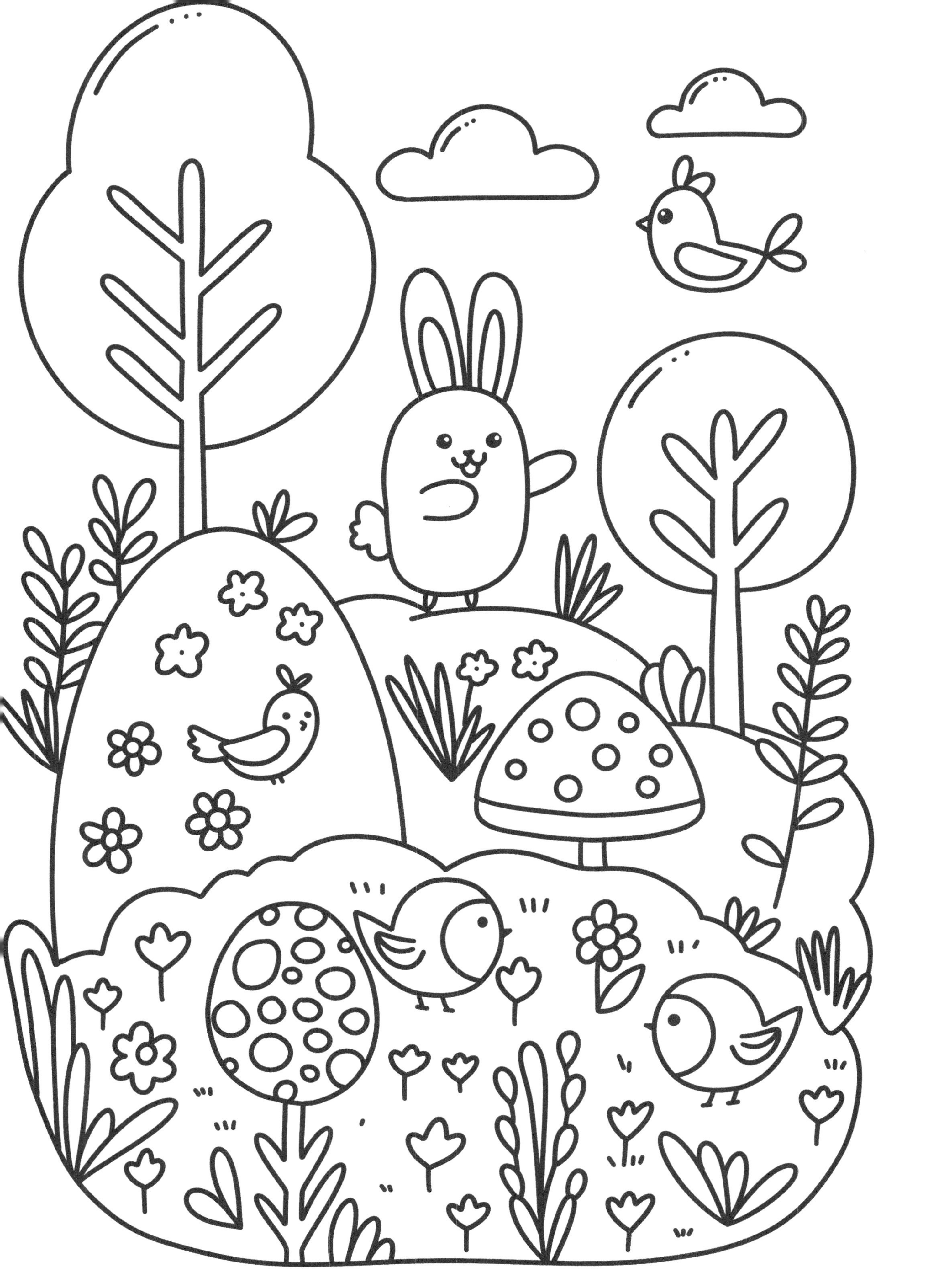

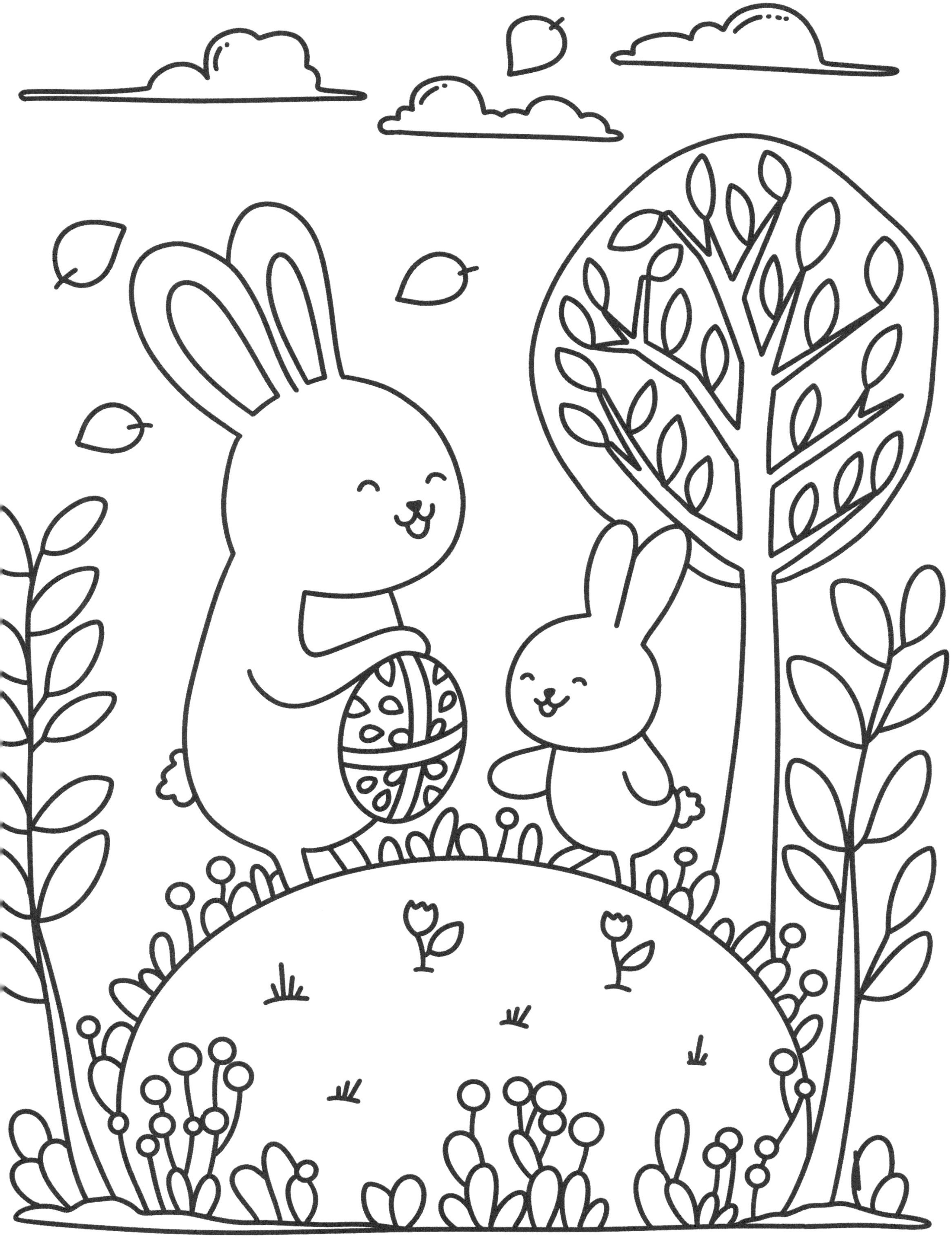

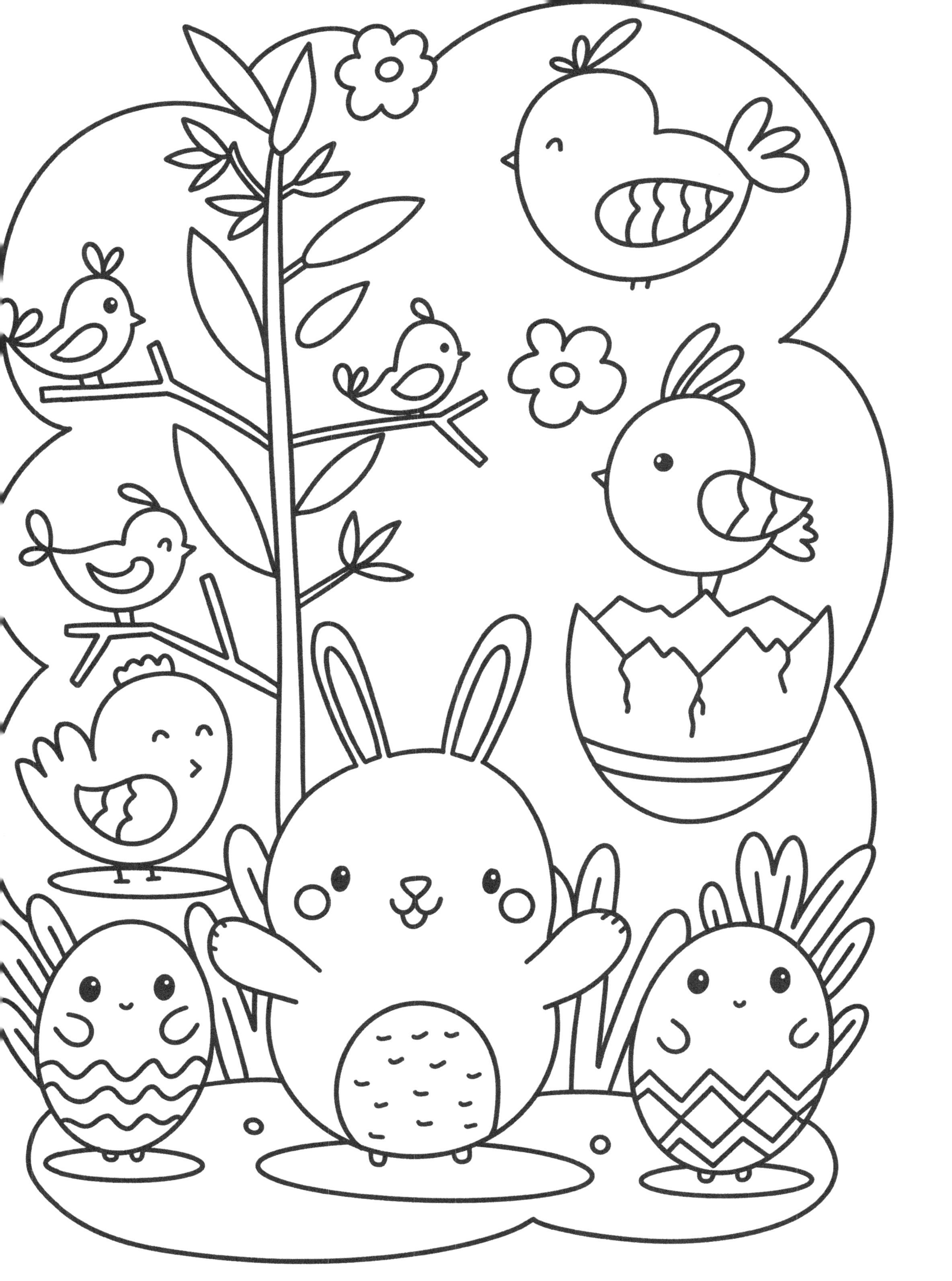

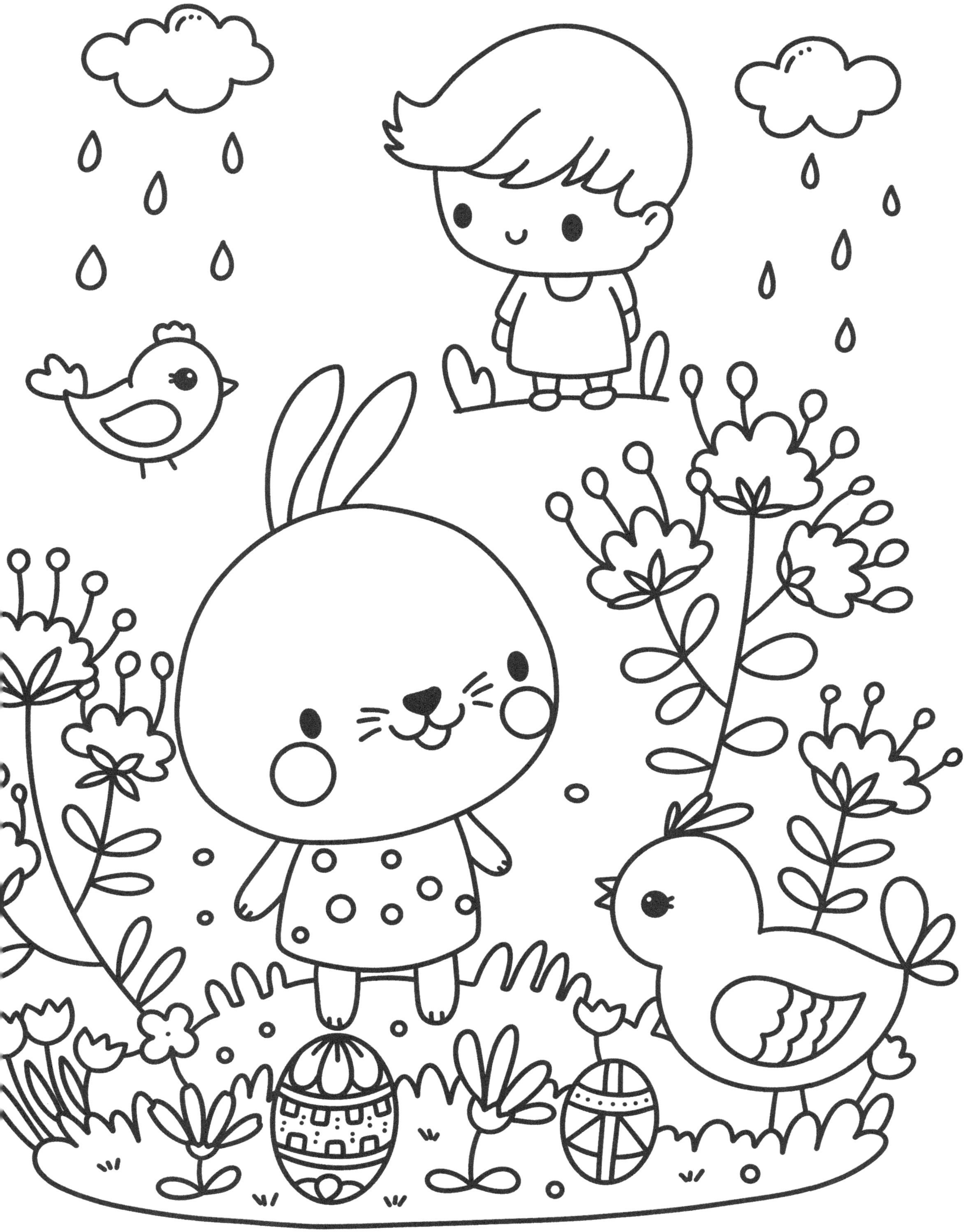

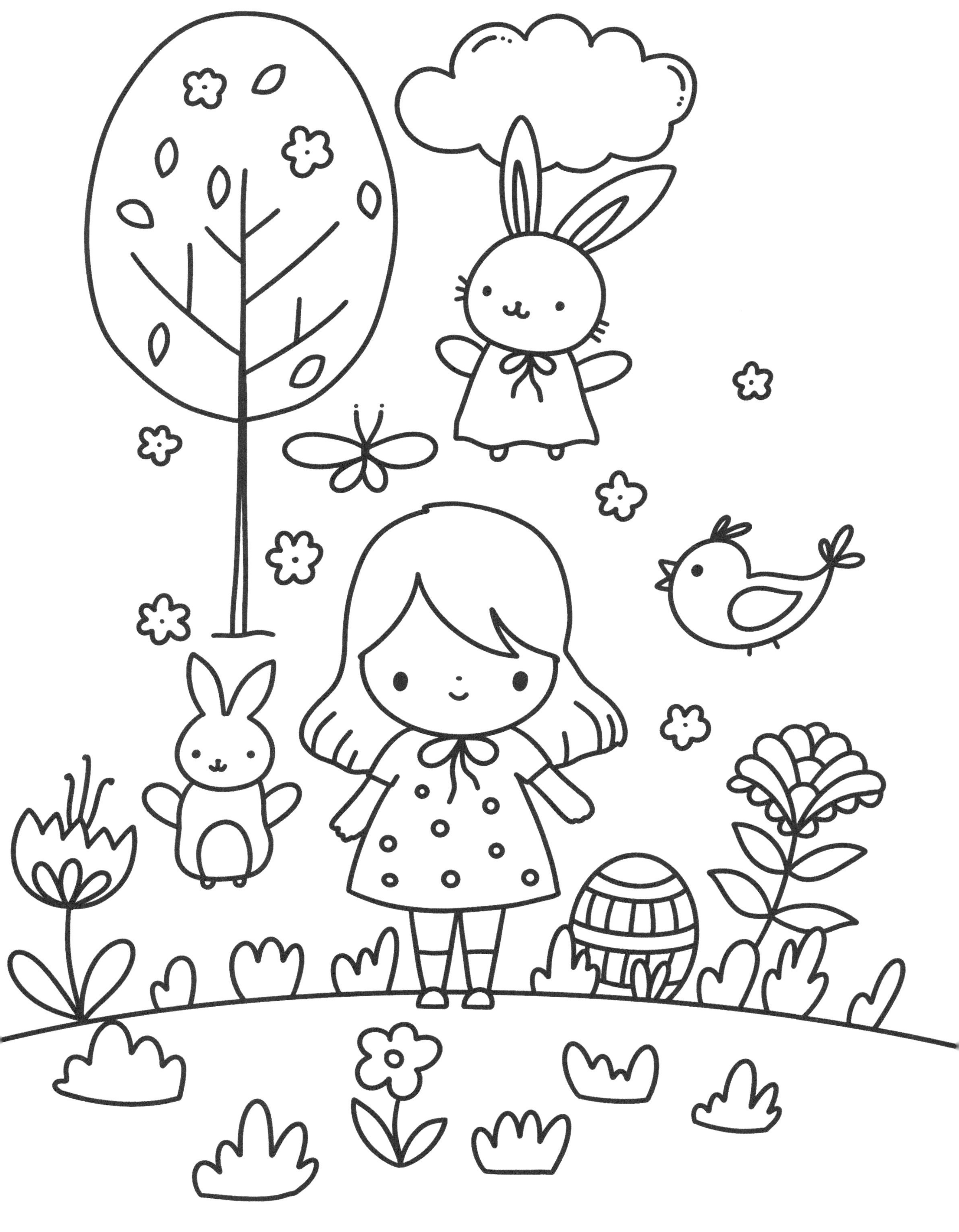

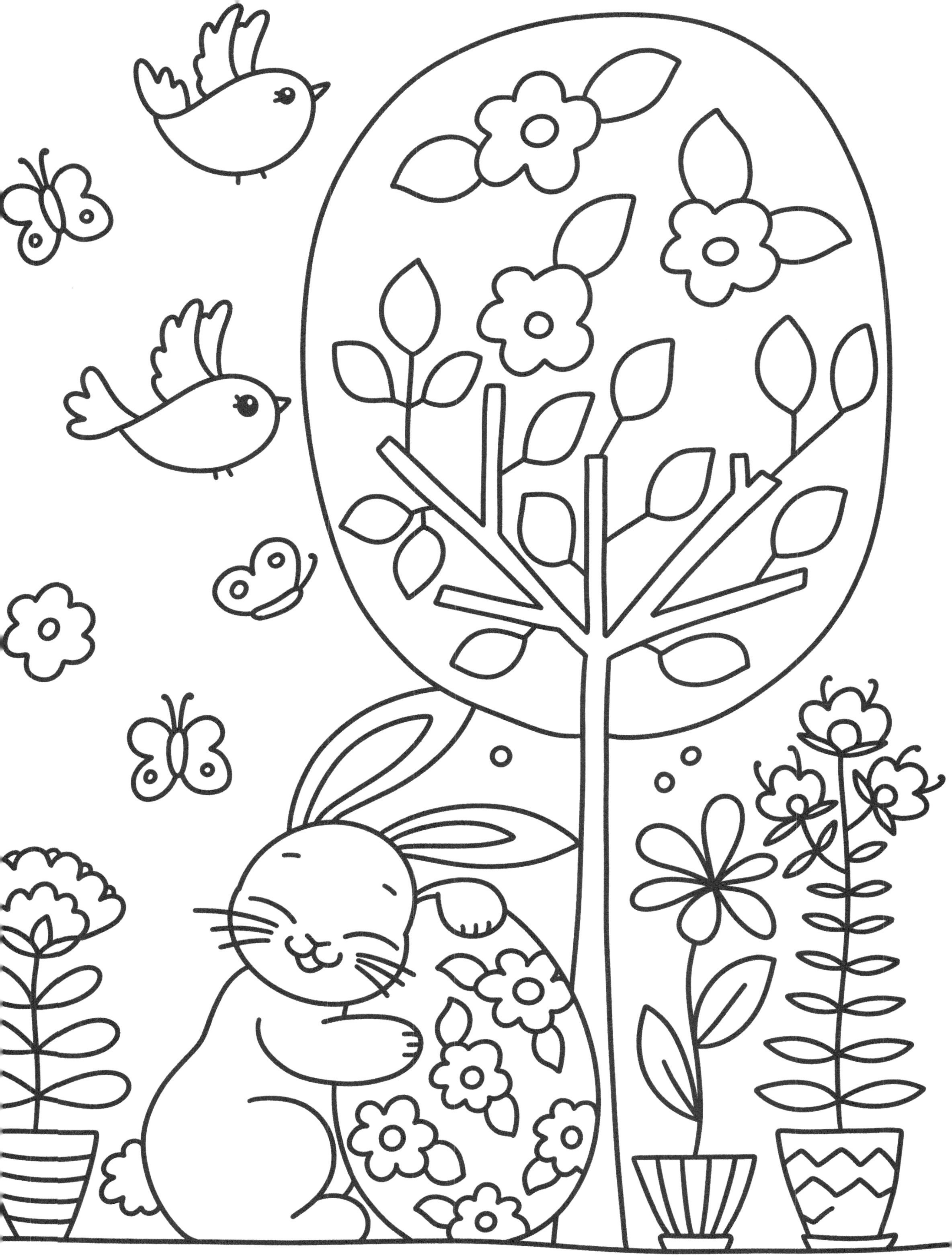

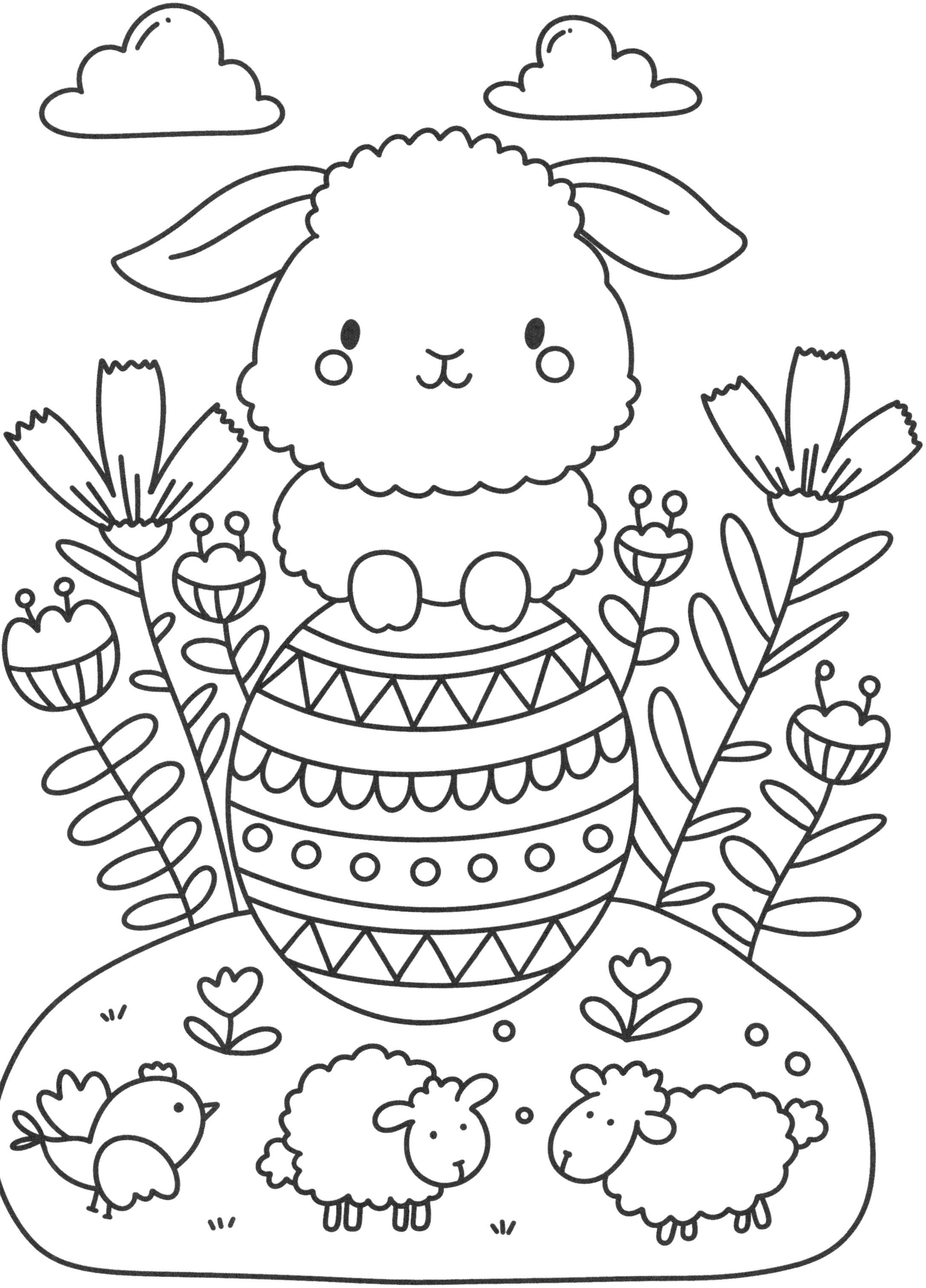

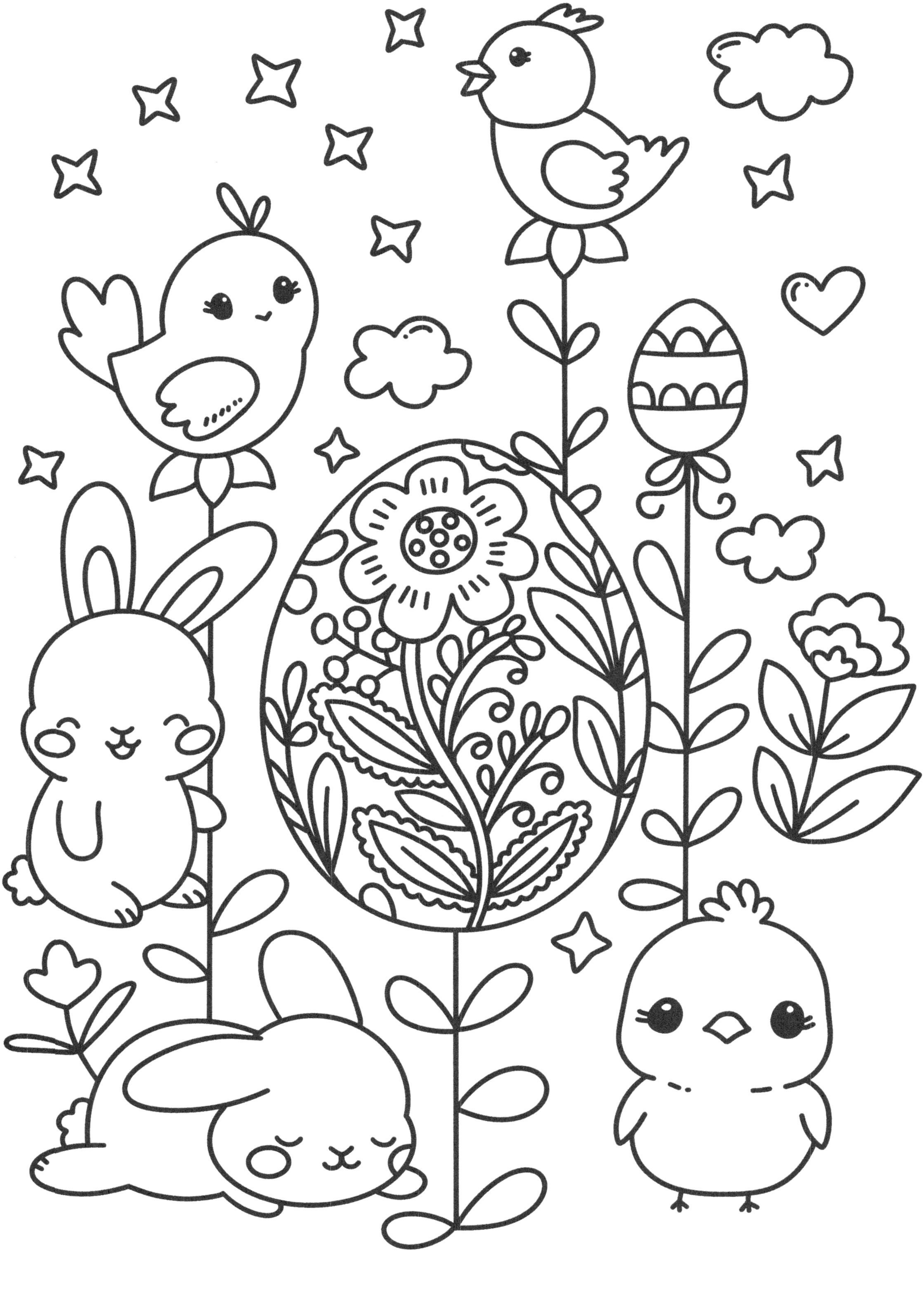

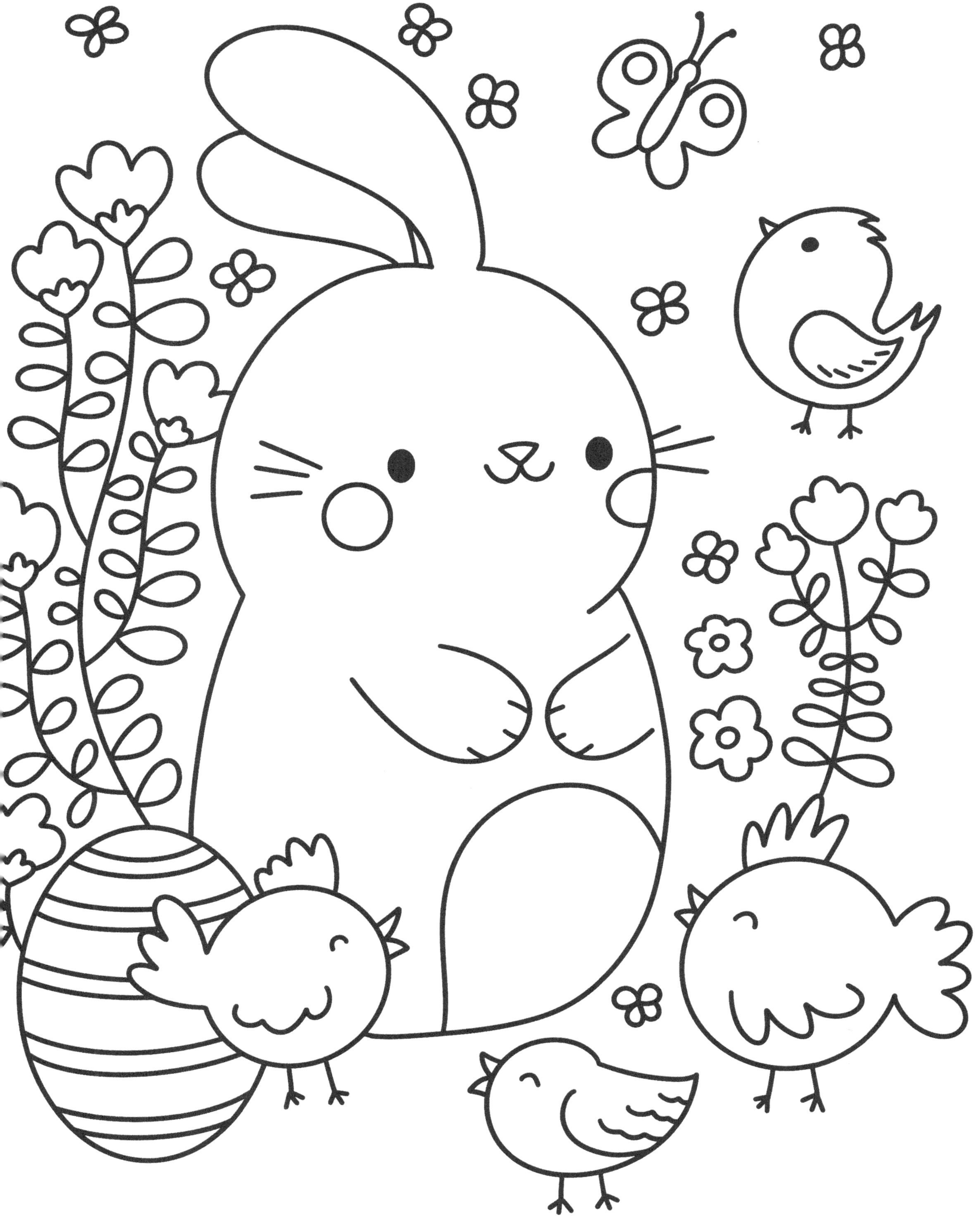

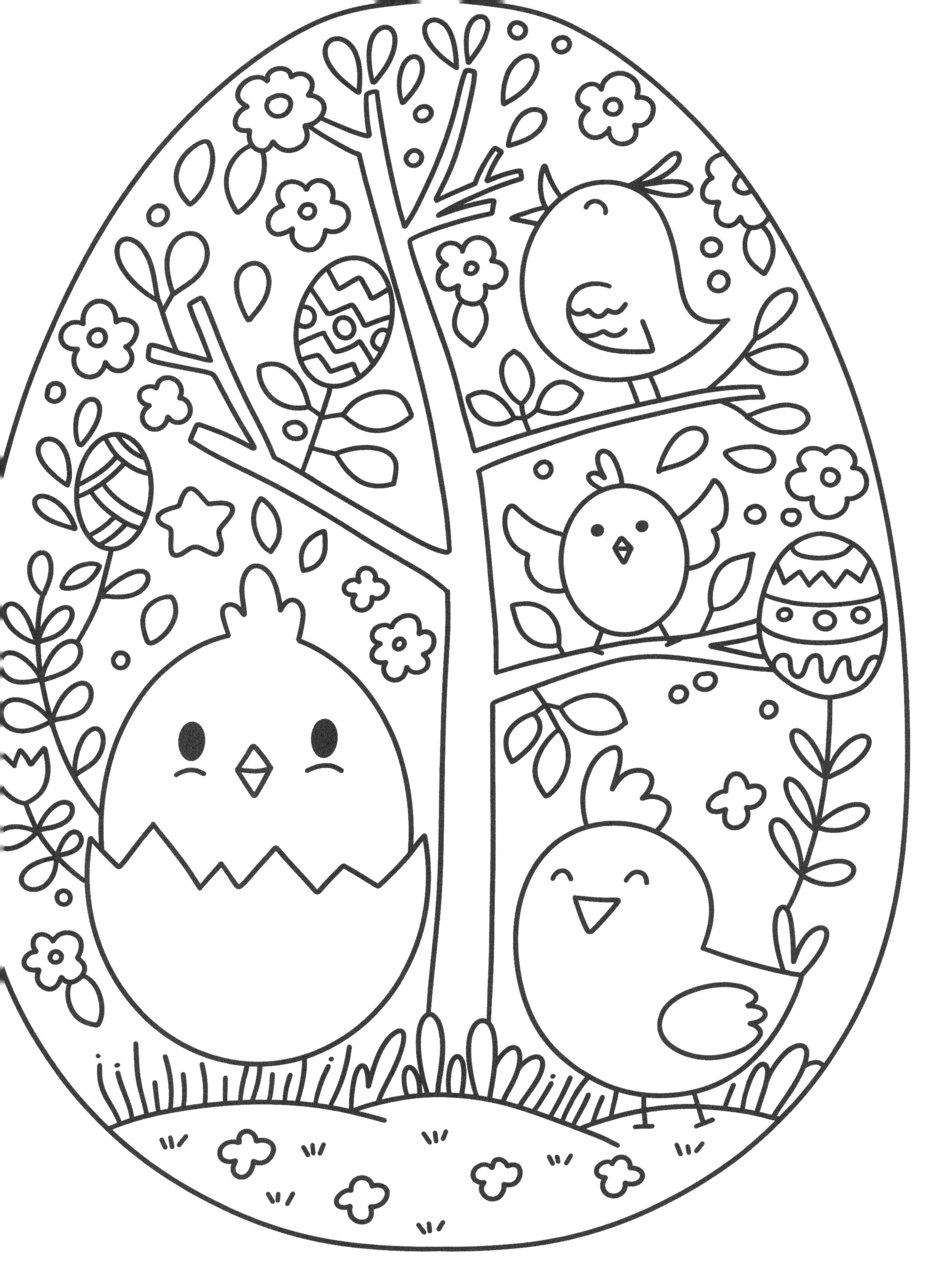

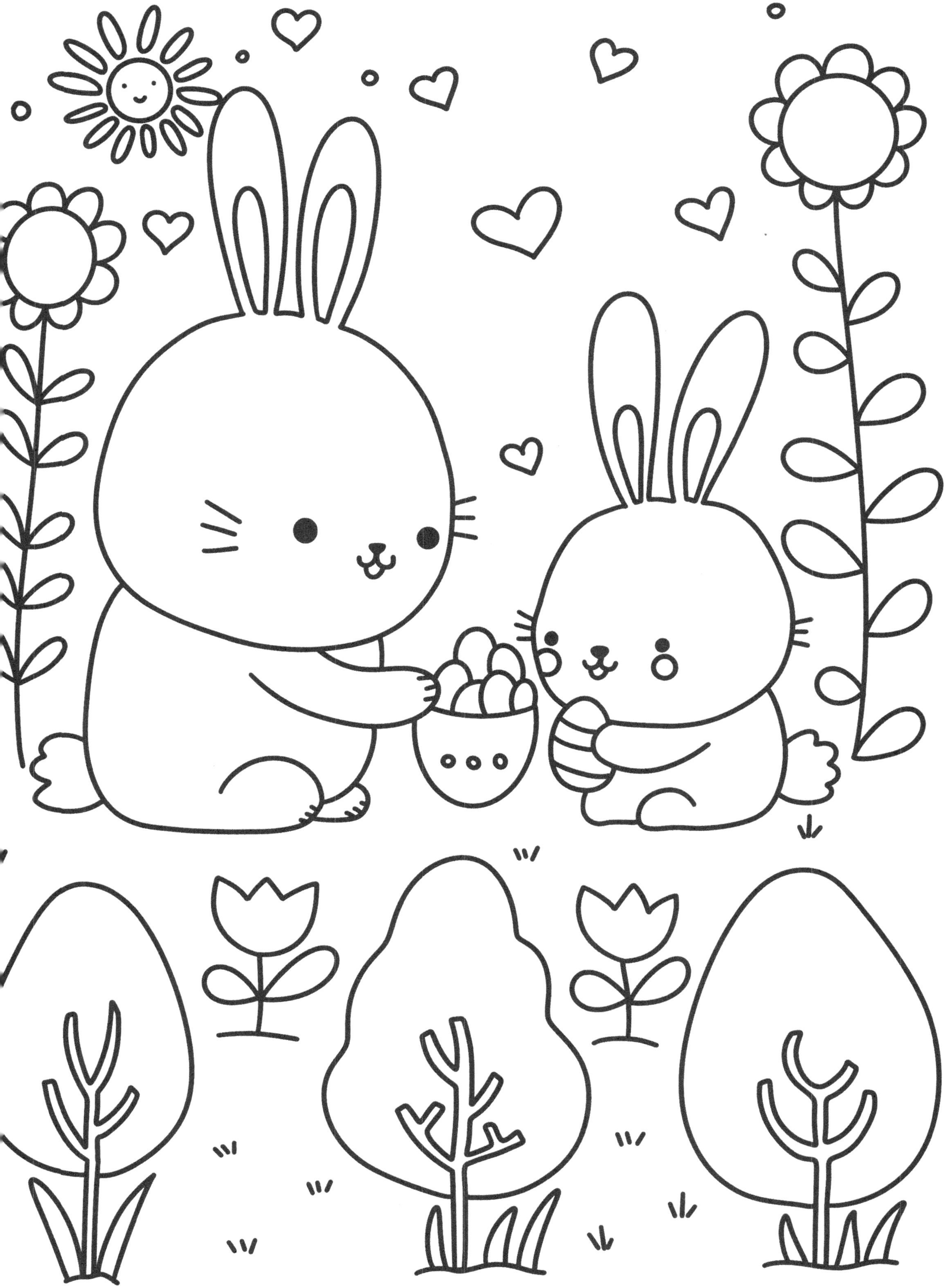

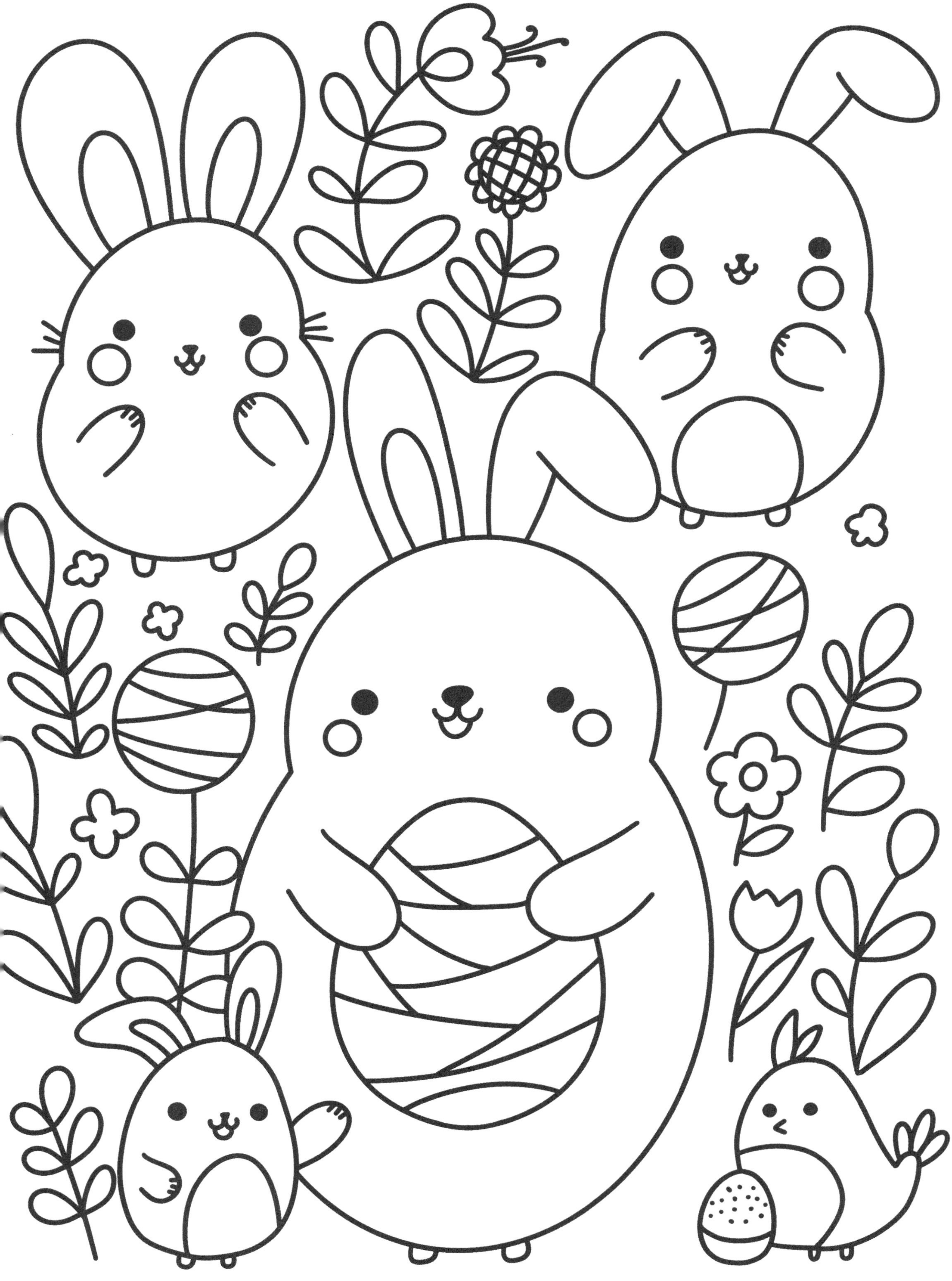

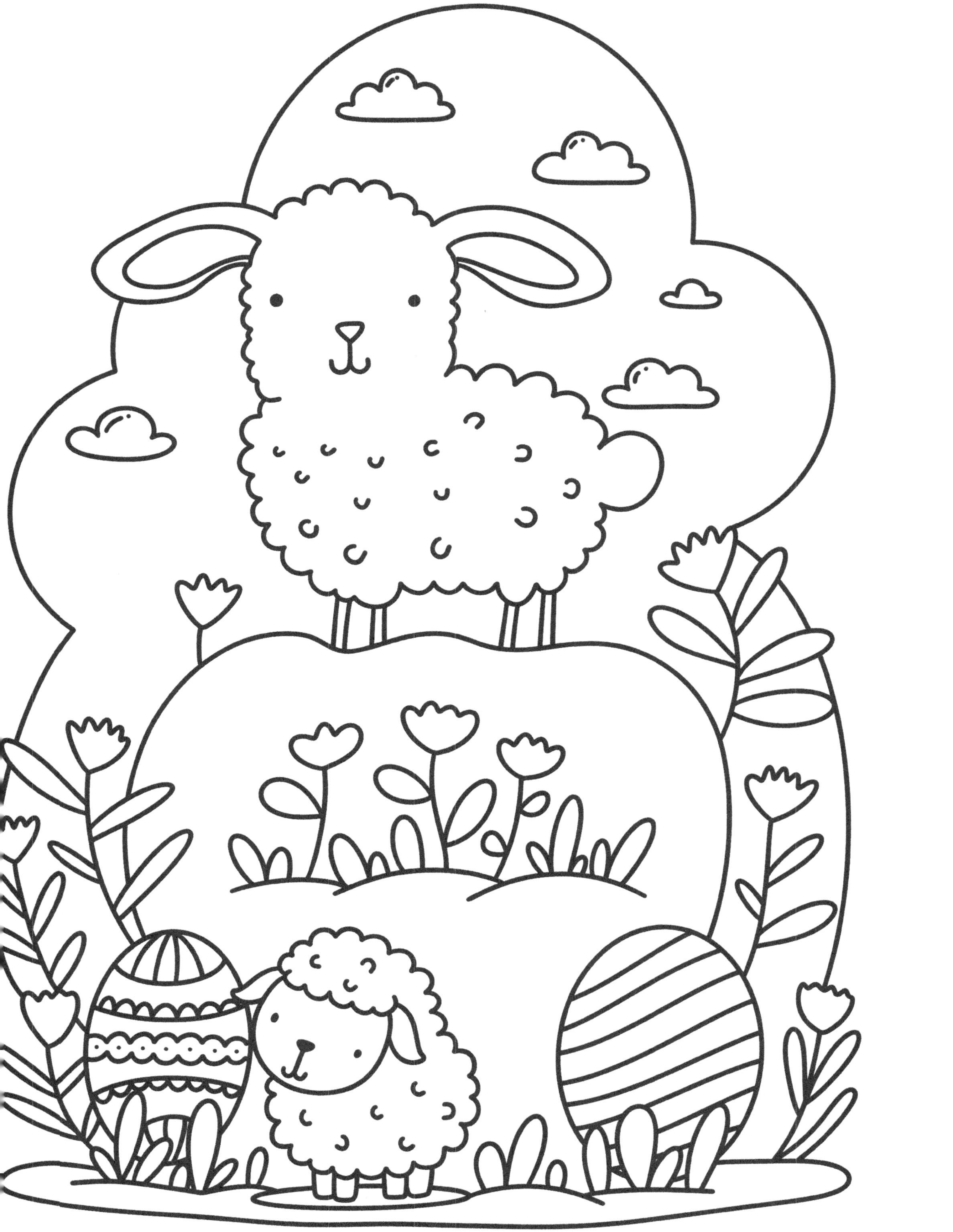

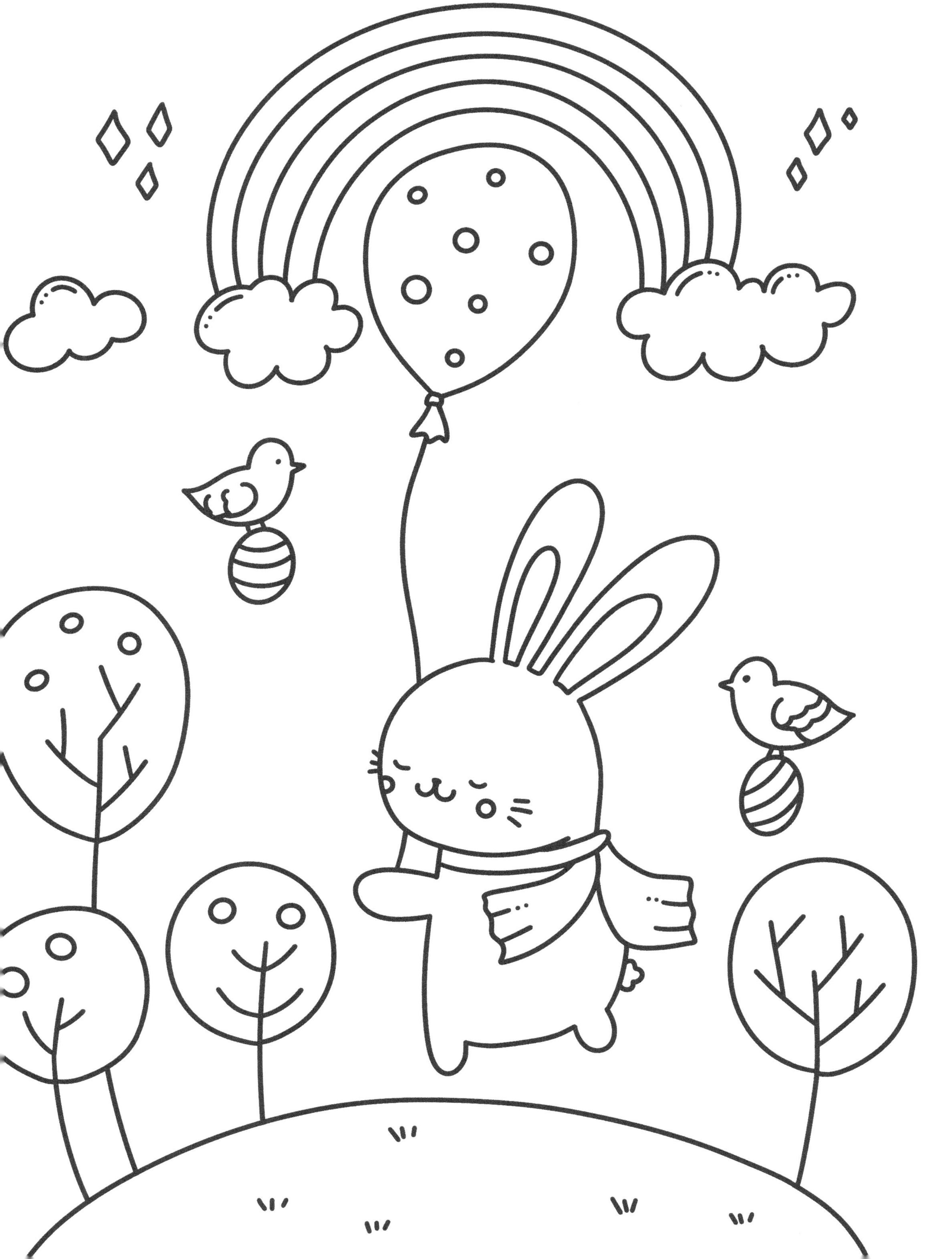

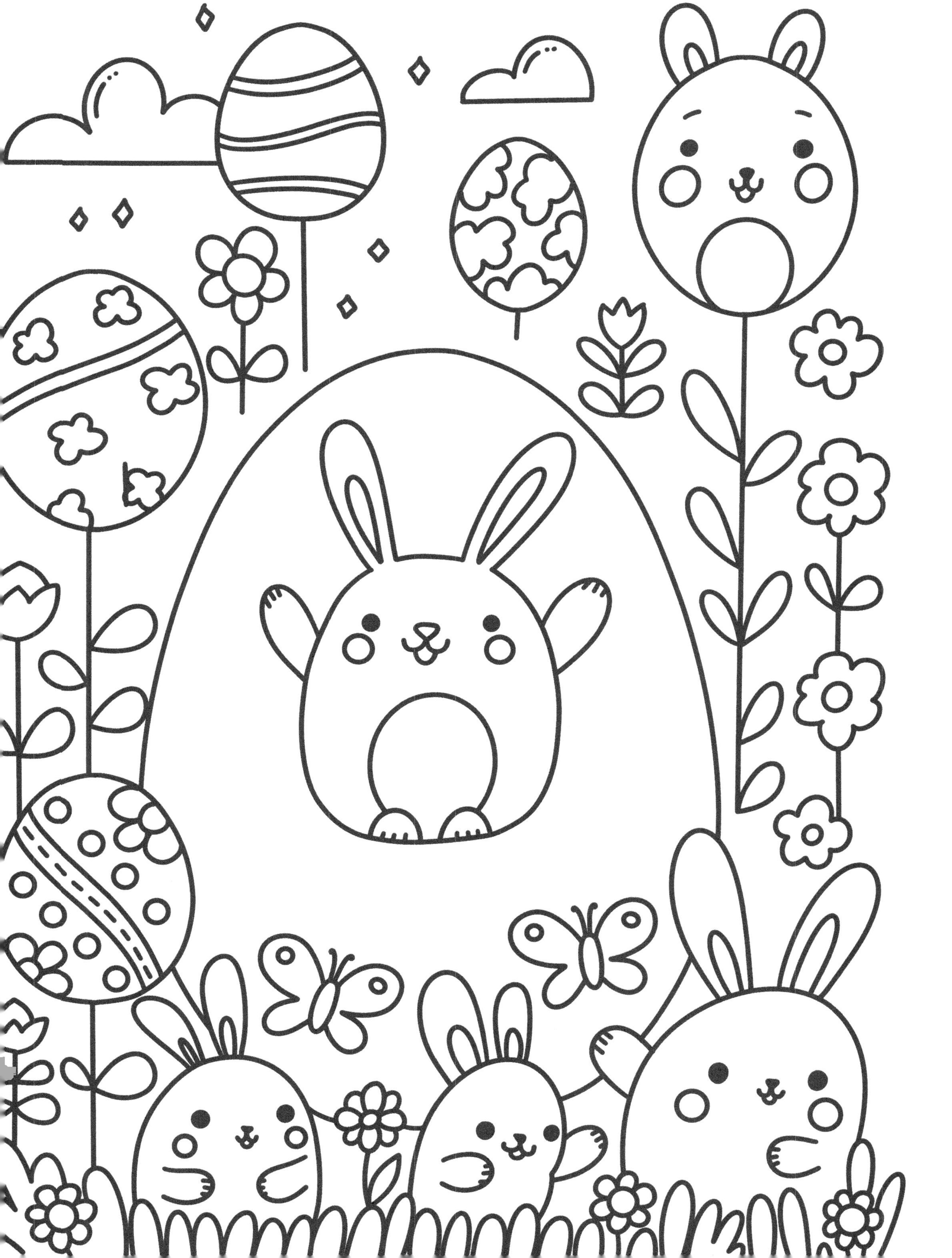

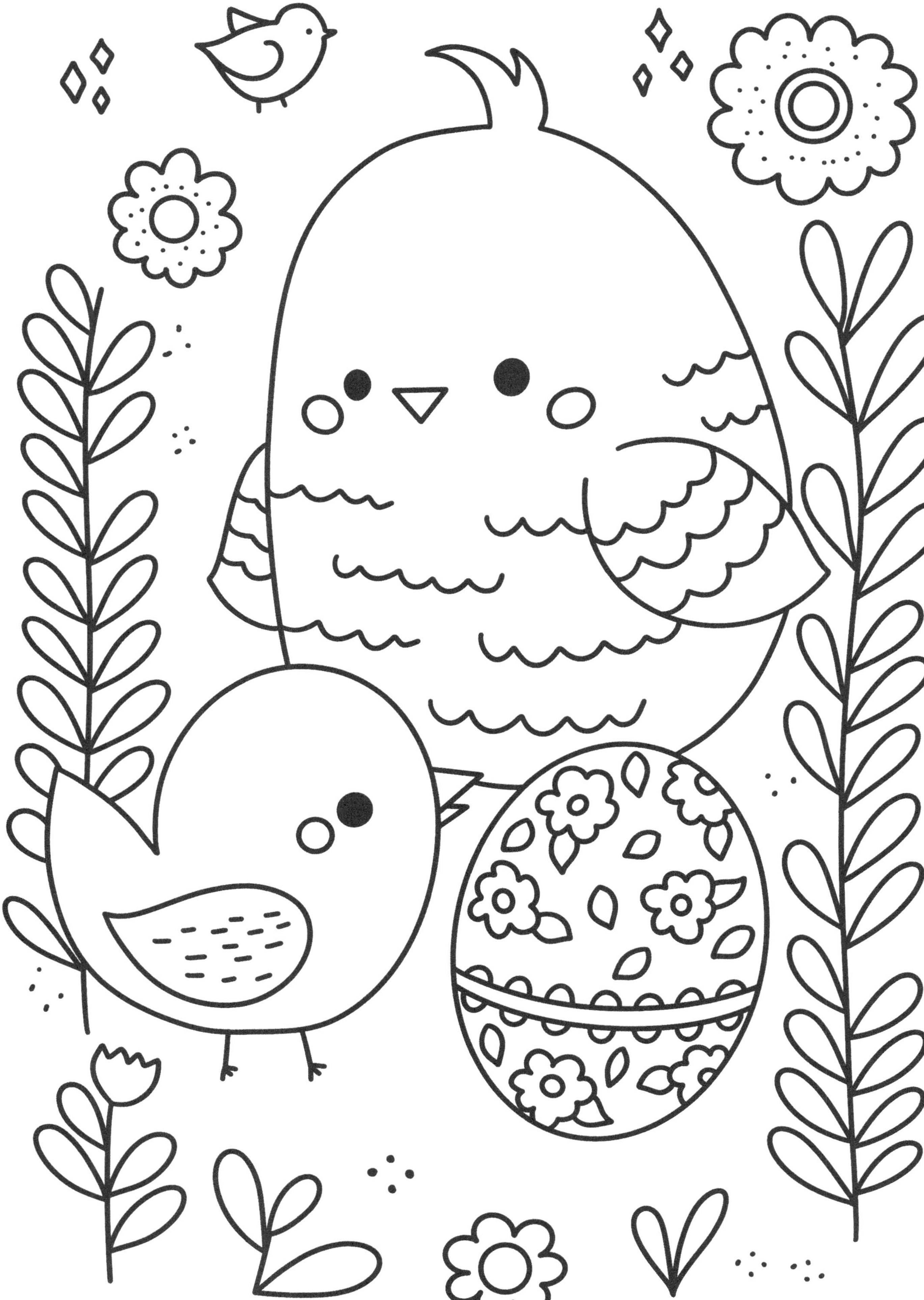

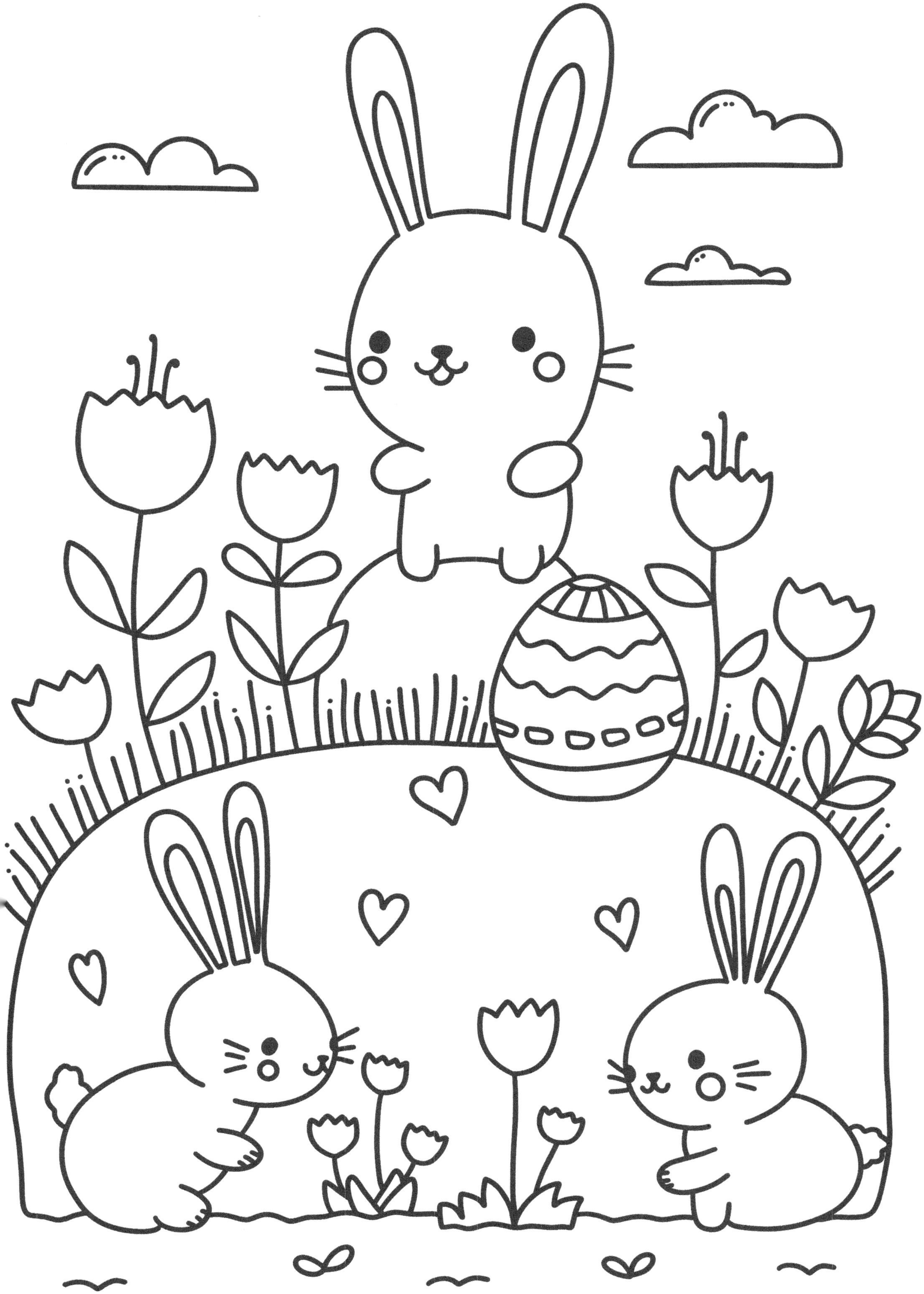

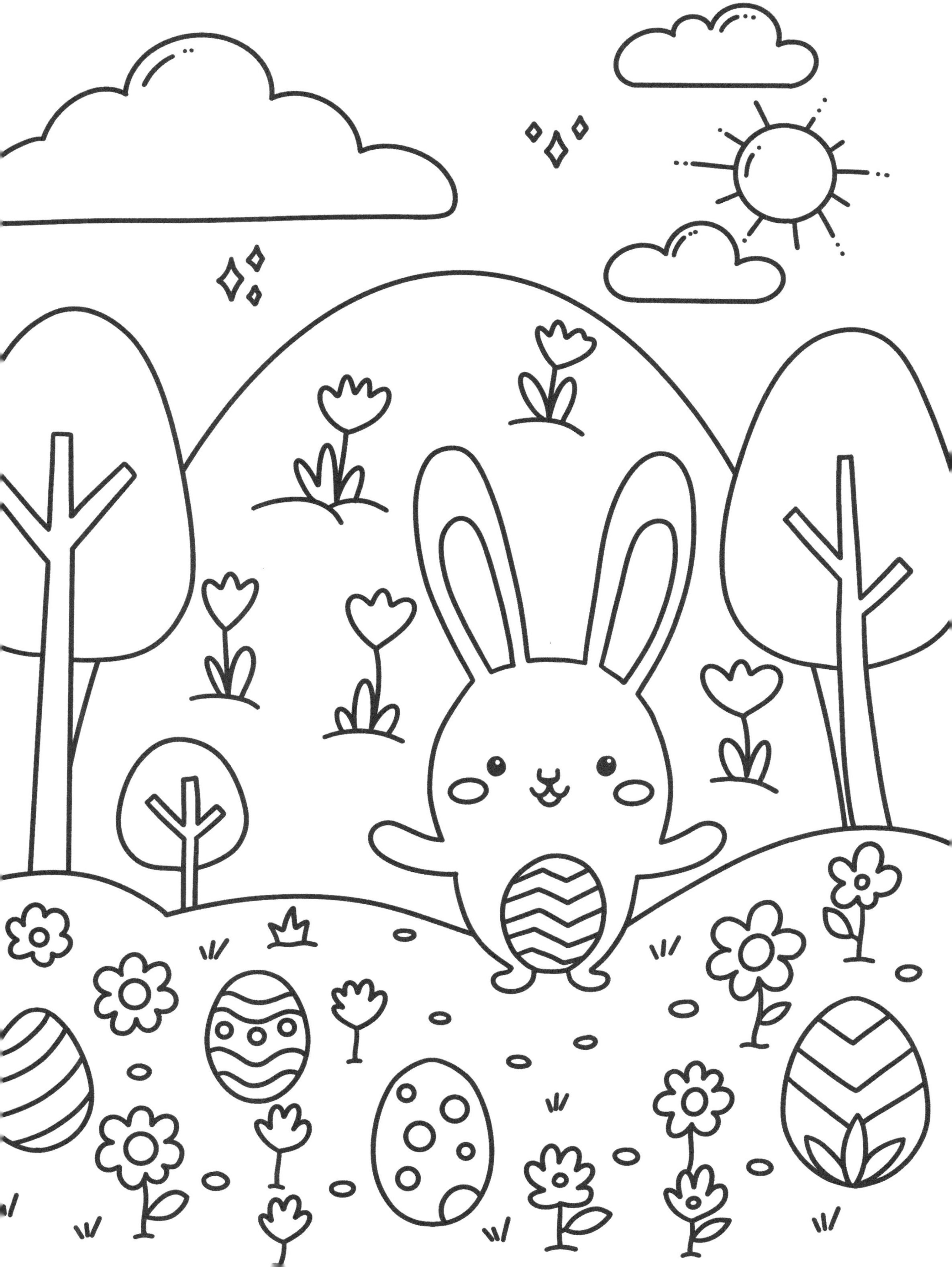

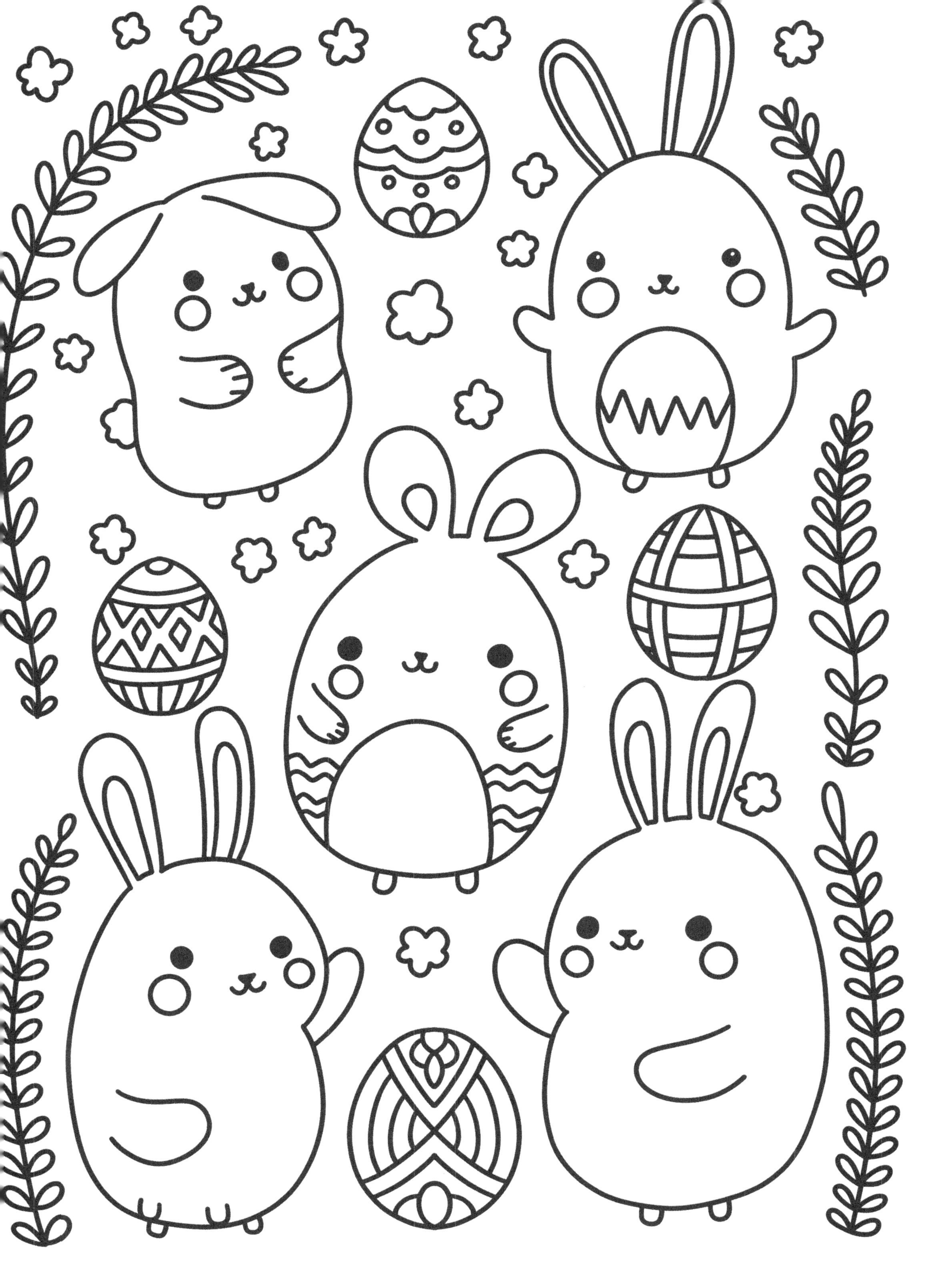

Made in the USA
Las Vegas, NV
15 March 2025

19601539R00031